SUBLIMATION

Khalilah Yasmin

Written by: Khalilah Yasmin

First Edition

Copyright © 2014 Khalilah Yasmin

All Rights Reserved.

ISBN-13: 978-0975396315
ISBN-10: 0975396315

Cover Art by: Mreeuh Chang

For Love, Muses, & Consciousness...

CONTENTS

GREAT EXPECTATIONS

CHILD'S PLAY

EMPATH

AFLAME IN A SHARP

KARMA

MISSED

HOW TO BE A B*TCH

SATAN'S KISS

THE GREATEST BLISS

MOUNT OLYMPUS

HER

HEAR ME, HERE ME

THIGH KEY

PERFECTION

SUBURBS

VERONICA

LOVE'S MOTHERF*CKER

LUCID DREAMER

SILENT SYMPHONY

LEZBEHONEST

DAMN

VERSE 6

IF I TOLD YOU

CRUISE

SYNCHRONICITY

STOCKHOLM SYNDROME

BASS

HAD

INFINITE LUST

MONSTER

UNICORN

DEAR YOU

BETWEEN BLINKS

AKA RICHARD

HAPPILY APATHETICALLY

MOAN

BROKEN GLASS

OMISSIONS

TANTRIC

THAT DAY

THE END

LIVE FOREVER

PUENTE HILLS

"That awkward moment when you're home alone in the shower and you feel someone tap you on the shoulder.

Aliens."

"Great Expectations"

What if I painted you the picture I wanted you to see?
Would you critique the aesthetic or allow it to be?

If I drew you a journey with both of my hands,
A possible existence and key to foreign lands.

What if this world were nothing but what the artists made it;
By believing there's diamonds in coals, and to never get jaded.

If I wrote you a song, that could only be heard through your eyes,
Would you crescendo visually and allow my notes to rise?

See, I, believe in the power of improvis—-ation.
The brush stroke and the guitar strum have the same connotation.

An image painted onto the mind of another;
A pixelated ladder into the abyss of wonder.

A stardust filled being to inspire and use,
To allow room for the unknown, the mystery of the muse.

To create a perspective perhaps otherwise neglected,

…As the greatest wonders of the world, are never expected.

"Child's Play"

I want to play with his toys and add myself to his collection,
Alter his erogenous zones; the reaction and stimulation to his erection.
His eyes like the ocean; deep, blue, and wet;
Piercing through my innocence and his I promise to protect.

I'm a flavor he has never had; a tunnel he has never dug,
My imagination foreshadows naked bliss when he pulls me into hug.
I long to make LOVE, he stares in the midst of his crowd,
His voice of me is silent but his eyes on me are loud.

But alas he is forbidden, and my subconscious intent and lust must be hidden.
As I heave for his kiss upon his mouth and his 'Vein Filled Bliss'.
Fantasizing myself into the depths of his blue ocean and his erection.

Cuming to his memory and careless thoughts without protection.
'Shakespeare's Two Headed Beast'- with a tiramisu complexion,
Wondering if he knows I've added him to my collection.

Like a child innocently eager to play with every single one of his toys,
Embracing him in fantasy is my reality, though he only likes boys.

"I absorb energy." "Oh, so you're like a Spiritual Tampon?"
"Yes... EXACTLY."

"Empath"

When you grew up like I did, you get really good at smiling and pretending that everything is okay.

You become really observant, feeling others simply by looking into their eyes, you hear the words they don't say.

You wonder if anyone is looking into your eyes, so with fear of being discovered you quickly look away.

You lay... in a ball of your own bull shit and wondering which past life made you this way.

When cocaine made it impossible to feel anything. I was okay back then. She made my heart race, and kept me up some nights but that 'white girl' was my friend.

She numbed the rejection of a family I once begged to love me or see that I existed.
She made me forget that I should have never let him fuck me,
when I made love the moment we kissed.

When you are criticized by acquaintances for not being Black enough because you enunciate your sentences,
but you're too Black for the casting or the front desk position because the Company President complained and said you were 'Too Ethnic'.

Staring into the moon, wondering which past life made me this way, when you're aware of your purpose, you know everything will be okay.

"It's good to get your ego crushed every once in a while. Your spirit feels lit aflame and suddenly you're reminded of your mortality."

"Aflame...in A Sharp" A#

Fear not deep waters or steep heights,
for passion is all of these things; whether you drown or free fall.

The muse told me to take advantage of this sadness before it passes,
to remind myself that I can feel.. to remember those before him as proof
that I can heal.

The muse promised that the burning beneath my ribcage was
temporary,
and that I should freely jump into the ocean again; even if it's scary.

Without a face or body, the muse whispered in my both of my ears at
the same time,
Forcing me to acknowledge the hidden message beneath the rhyme.

Soaking my psyche into the world of wonder that exists beyond the end,
the ego that silenced her voice and pretended to be his friend.

Tricking myself to hide vulnerability because if I lost myself too long,
by staring into the sheet music, I would become the note and not the
song.

The desire that won't extinguish but yet has been lit aflame,
Like an angel lit on fire jumping into the waterfall surrounded by terrain.

Although doused by the waterfall and submerged in its depth;
My wings still full of fiery passion,
And my chest of strong heavy breaths.

*"Take advantage and fan the flames
as they will not burn you into ash-but instead make you seen from light years away."*

The muse whispered in my ears, so I promised to fly and not to lay.
To not trick myself into hiding my truth, allow myself to get lost because it is never wrong,
Wings on fire as I stare into a memory, No longer the note. I am the song.

"Be courteous to everyone. You never know who you'll end up in a locked elevator with..."

"Karma"

You're a born asshole and I fuckin' hate you.

I wish 8, 9, 10, niggas would hold you down and rape you.
Then cut you, ...and pour gasoline in all your orifices;
This once sweet girl has now gone thru metamorphosis.

I'm bad now, I'm evil, and I wish A MUTHA Would-
go toe to toe with you now, I betchu I could.
I sent your ass roses, and never got a damned flower,
licked you in secret places, and got wild in the shower.

BUT FOR WHAT? For you to be ungrateful, and throw at me SHIT,
My Good Karma did me no good, if this is what I get.
Got me in the grocery store on the phone swearing,
had me in the hospital dehydrated, that's how much I was caring,

Crying myself to sleep, lack of food and didn't want to eat.
You were the wolf when I was the sheep!
You made me think you loved me, I fell for that shit
My good Karma did me no good, if YOU were what I'd get.

As the gasoline burns thru your orifices, and your insides are swole

I throw my lit blunt, cheers to you, you fuckin' ASSHOLE.

"Missed"

I don't miss you, I miss who you pretended to be,
and since pretending isn't real- I miss nothing at all.

I haven't changed my number, yet subconsciously wait for your call.

You see, I thought I was a dreamer, until my dream was deferred.
I thought I was a poet, until your presence created my words.

But if that was your representative, imitation of what you knew I wanted to see,
I cannot miss 'YOU' and who you pretended to be.

But I miss me. I miss me before I knew that my dream could exist.
I miss being naive, I miss me being kissed.

A sincere embrace that now has become a mirage,
the colored stain glass now a tainted collage.

I thought I was awake, but I realize it was a dream
And even in my nightmares I'm forbidden to scream.

My mouth is open, yet silent,

My body shaking like thunder. Violent-ly...

I don't miss you... I guess I miss me.

"How to be a B*tch"

You silence me when you think I've said too much.
Yet I'm a bitch if you reach and I don't want your touch.
A bitch when I'm honest instead of telling a lie,
I'm typical when I have emotion and start to cry.
I'm too deep because you're too shallow to understand,
You think I'm strange and failed to realize I don't give a got damn.
I entered this universe on this trip with one goal this time,
I'm going to live for me, cause my life is MINE.

I'm needy if I show you that I love you too much,
Yet I'm a bitch if I scowl because you forced your hand's touch.

I'm a fag, I'm a dyke, because you don't see things the same,
you're a commi, you're a dick, and you're all the same.
I'm a freak, if I speak descriptively in erogenous terms,
I'm a prude if I decide that I don't want your germs.

I'm going to hell because I do not believe in "your" God,
I'm a heathen if I believe in spirituality and think religion is odd.

I'm too sweet when ran over by a certain type of man,
I have class, and I do not want your ring on my hand.
A bitch when I'm honest when you'd rather I lie,
A good girl gone better and I'll tell you why;

You broke me to the bottom with your ignorance and hate,
I rose a new person, impervious to adversity late.
Ashamed I once was to be considered too strong,
Until your words made me weak, and lasted too long.
If strong is a bitch, then that is to you who I will be,
When you see me lifting mountains, and flying freely.

I may not be wealthy, but with much I am rich,
I thank you sincerely for teaching me "HOW- TO- BE -A-BITCH".

"Satan's Kiss"

As temptation led me, and my heart followed your path,
added desire, love, and lust, to an evil trail of math.

The offer you held in your hand, was a gift and a curse,
upon approaching you I recited bible verses.
For no one rehearses the day they give away their soul,
and all they have to offer to a heart that was cold.

And I like a child, who had been lured down this maze,
saw the sweets that you held, intrigued I fell in a daze...
I wanted to play, in your Pandora's Box,
fascinated with glee, to run my fingers through your locks.
You sly as a fox, and I was your rabbit,
as if I approached you naked and allowed you to grab it.
I wanted you to have it, and ignored the snakes in your eyes,
ignorance is bliss yet in my case, I forced a disguise.

I pretended your evil ambitions were in my imagination,
for yours was the touch that led to my masturbation.
So you had my mind, before you had my body,
stringing my heart into your celebration.

All of my possessions I laid out before you,
and as I watched you hurt me, I still couldn't help but adore you.
Who are you? I asked myself inside of my mind,
willingly donating my pussy, and leaving all else behind.

Fascinated with glee to run my fingers through your locks,
open arm, wide nosed to play in your Pandora's Box.
Lord could have warned me, of your gift and your curse.
Searching my mind with prayer as I now again, recite bible verse.
I pretended I didn't see the danger for ignorance was my bliss,
I fell a fool to you forever, for you gave me Satan's Kiss.

"The Greatest Bliss"

Feeling worthless when I know I'm worth it.
This too shall pass as I pray it passes soon.

I'm losing weight and don't have much weight to lose.
I'm losing myself because I let my heart be used.

The greatest bliss was outdone by the greatest devastation.
My abstinent investment in exchange for humiliation.
This too shall pass and I pray it passes soon.
I'm losing weight and don't have room to lose.

I'm losing myself as I stand surrendered in front of God.
I felt cupid's arrow. Suffered through the puncture of the rod.

No drug or drink can escape me from myself.
Feeling worthless and I'm the only one who can help.

You prayed WITH me and thanked God that I existed.

Your beliefs don't match your behavior.
Where's the God in this?

"Mount Olympus"

I said I wouldn't do this but here I am.

I promised myself not to give any f*cks so instead I gave 3 damns.

Man.

Here I stand, with one foot in my mouth and the other in your hand.

Flexibility... has me floating in the sea of my own contradiction,

Staring into your eyes then down at my own crucifix-ion...

Between my breasts as my heartbeat rejoices upon your lips

between my Mount Olympus,

I hunger for your pleasure, while we pray we never finish.

Your steel rope is my lasso, I'm a slave to your noose,

pleasure asphyxiated praying you won't let me...

loose-n the exasperated hold on your d*ck...

It's warm and it's thick, and I remember none before it,

I want to feed it, love it, choke it, as you let me adore it.

I've explored it. This place inside me that I tried to keep hidden,

Insatiably at your disposal with my own nipples bitten.

Erotica; another planet that you take me,

when your breath reaches my air,

You; my beautiful addiction, I'm your nymph, You; my satyr.

"HER"

Death is NOT, the worst thing contrary to popular belief,

Love is a empty path with a dungeon beneath.

Being shot if chosen, versus having your heart shatter,

I'd take the bullet, and watch my brain splatter.

Oh what's the matter? I'm sick of being hurt,

Wear my heart on my sleeve, I PLASTERED it on my shirt!

Once this love is over, I've chosen the dungeon for my home,

Be loved, romanced, then screwed, (pause) I'd rather be alone...

Black is NOT, the deepest of darkness that exists...

It's loving him exquisitely and watching him kiss...

HER.

"Sometimes you must run away and hide, just to see who gives enough of a sh*t to come find you." – 'Bin Laden'

"Hear ME, HERE me"

I'm dealing with cards that someone else gave me,
searching for an answer, and there's nothing to save me..

I fall,

I fall,

I reach for a hand that's not there...
There's nowhere to turn to, my life seems so unfair...
I've forgotten how to cry because HE told me I cried too much,
but didn't realize I cried as well, when he leaned in to touch.
Fuck, Looking in my closets at the demons I pretend to not see,
I ignore them all day, yet I know they see me.

I'm saving a LIFE, that someone else gave me,
I'm a torn wild mess, with nothing to tame me.
But solstice and silence where my heart beats so loud,
I can hear it beat through my body through the drums of a crowd.
I'm strong but I'm weak, I shut up while I speak,
Holding in what you pushed away, when you hurt me that day...

Watching my world tear down before me,
You want me to smile because you pretend to adore me,
YOU BORE ME.
There's more to me, that you ever bothered to find,
I gave you my most prized, my high, I gave you my mind.

I'm fighting a war that someone else gave me,
because I'm still alive, you point and you blame me.
I'm ashamed see, because I don't want to feel so strong,
how can someone be so hurt for so long?

How is everyone even down to even her kin,
the rejection she feels in a heart born in sin.

I fall,

I fall,

reaching for a hand that's not there
I want to run, but to another emptiness? WHERE?

Living in a world, where we fend for ourselves,
I fall
I fall,
Born alone, and still by myself.

Seeing a reflection of peace but a heart that is weary,
I'm crying inside, and no one can hear me.

"Thigh Key"

Art defined; a skill or experienced evolved trait,
Mastered, appreciated, and well worth the wait.

Caution to your wind, that blew my body and soul beyond my mind,
Liberty and freedom capturing me, a victim, premonition; elusively blind.

The more I resisted, the more I longed to be chased,
Hungry for my own thirst, and the imagining taste.
Lace, in comparison, is the thrill that you gave me,
Between the intricate fibers, glimpses of skin wanted you to save me.

Take my body as the ocean takes the waves and make me drown,
Desire possessed my every thought calculating your specific shade of brown...

Resisting, in body, and morale that became a religion,
Accepting your taboo with time, and your needle to my incision.

I made the decision, let you be the Master to my puppet,
Erogenous zones anticipating temptations to covet.
I deny, and I love it, for I am succumbing to and becoming the bait,
Releasing my own pleasures in my imagination, to prepare for my fate.

My limbs no longer satisfy me, for I am allured,
Feverishly craving your juice to drink me to cured.
Drawn in by a *connection* that blind sighted my psyche,
Attempting to silence my thoughts while singing to Lykke.
Stirred with confusion and discontented, afraid of what this might be...
Aroused in intellect, controlling my body as I gave you my thigh key.

You unlocked my mind, so I gave you my treasure,
and since that moment, there has been no greater pleasure.
I made the decision, let you be the Master to my puppet,
Erogenous zones anticipating temptations to covet.

Drawn in by a connection that blind sighted my psyche,
aroused in intellect, body and mind as I gave you my *thigh key*.
Captured the right victim, whom lusted for the abduction,
For now I am a slave, to the "Art of Seduction" ….

"Perfection"

I wanted you to be my canvas,
I breathe art, philosophy, poetically ...

And You wanted an ass to kiss, literally...

I want something deeper than something that wants to go deep IN me.
I want a connection, and nothing like what all the other men be
When they want the panties without the romancing,
The grinding without the perpetual dancing.

I want the fairy tale.
And I promise I will get it.
I don't believe in perfection, I believe we can split it.

'Mr. Right' may come before I am ready.
'Mr Right Now' is wrong-
'Mr Happy Medium' can have me.

Allow us to paint together and use one another's brushes,
I want this to be stronger than any of my crushes.

I've lusted, and promise there's a difference.
To have love in the moment and love that's infinite,

A LIFE WITHIN IT
By it I mean the air we breathe within each others kiss.
Upon one another lips- not just another ass to kiss..
literally.
Because I see with the eyes that no one else can find.
I see within my soul, a girl like me, she sees with her mind.
While you think I'm blind and dumb witted, I'm paying attention and quick when I spit it.
When I'm silent I'm observing the most,
And when I've ceased to exist, I don't leave a ghost.

I want to be your lover, but your name is not Prince and I am not 'cuming'
For you to know my screams in your psyche BEFORE I start humming.

My theories may chase you away,
and though I don't plan for forever,
I put a purpose to my today... so if you want to stay...
I'm sure within this subliminal only few will get it.
I don't believe in perfection... but I believe we can split it.

"Suburbs"

Today's another holiday;
Everyone around me cheery and excited.
I face my fate with apprehension
not thankful to be invited.
For this is my twenty-fourth Christmas,
and nothing has changed;
He knows my birthday
yet my own father mispronounces my name.
Surrounded by a room of strangers
whom look just like me,
they share stories and pictures,
but no memory of me.

For this is only Christmas,
third time seeing "Dad" this year,
my sadness becomes anger
so "why am I here?"
Conversation with me scripted,
so I stopped answering the phone,
He never tried to know me
I grew up alone.
But hey I turned out pretty awesome
and my favorite color is blue.
Your gift of verse passed down to me,
and I look just like you.
Today, Yesterday, and may be your twin stranger forever,
I've lost interest in your family tree, and spending time together.
Because I called you in tears
when I was twenty five,
Thanks Dad for only being concerned
whether I was alive.
You should know my dreams,
and that you were my tears,
I wanted to have you like "THEY DID"
for so many years.
But you tucked me away in the 'suburbs'
I never had a family,
I've accepted this finally, as I walk away gladly.
Instead of being surrounded by a room of strangers,
and a Dad more concerned with his other six;
I kept it at the top but now I'm removing you from my one life wish...
I'm moving away, and you'll only know when you find this poem,
don't bother finding me, for I'm happy, and want to be left alone.
I tried to talk to you, you didn't want to hear my plea,
You; my father, and a stranger that looks just like me.

"VERONICA"

I don't want to but,
she says that I must.
If I come near you,
my windows she promised to bust.
Her words; I trust,
knowing she is sincere.
I kiss you like an addict
as you lay here.
And I am in need
I fiend for my fix,
as she stands outside my mansion,
hand bouncing a brick.
I put up with her shit;
as we inhale the same enamored air.
Ignoring her presence
as if we don't care.
But we do-we are lost
in another borrowed moment,
She's screaming our names
as I tell you, "you own it."
Your kisses were slow,
and now like rain they pour,
I pull your frame towards me,
you beg me for more.
"She will kill me
and make you watch me die,"
We laugh at reality,
your smile grazing my thigh.
You lay in my bosom,
as we share all our dreams,
I clap off my lights
as she shrieks and she screams
You lean in to kiss me,
and give me my fix,
Silence replaced with broken glass,
as in comes her Brick.

"I guess the real reason I couldn't date an athlete is; I always see them in the news strangling their girlfriends...

and... I have a long neck."

"Love's MotherF*cker"

Maybe if I hate LOVE, LOVE will finally LOVE me.

I've loved LOVE for too long and it seems to hate me.

LOVE pretends to LOVE me until I have completely surrendered.

LOVE says all the right things and then forgets to remember.

LOVE likes to chase me, when my back is to the eye,

by the time I have turned around and made LOVE earn me, LOVE is goodbye.

But why? I was a LOVE child wasn't I?

Shouldn't love be easy for me... or are my expectations met with a lie.

I thought I had a rock, and it turned into sand...

Slipped out of my grasp, between the fingers of my hands.

I don't want to cry. I just want to feel what I put out when I LOVE another.

LOVE- I want to hate you... you've been a sorry shit.

LOVE? -You mother fucker.

"Lucid Dreamer"

Even though; it has been months since I last kissed your face.
Even if I cried silently during our last warm embrace..
Even though; you never loved me back, I never loved another more.
Even if you were my heart, and treated me like your whore.

I loved you.

I loved you passed my heart, in places passed my mind.
I loved you deeply in places I wish that I could still find.

For if I could find the place in me that my love resides;
I'd dig and remove you and each thread, you left behind
But I find, you... waiting for me in my sleep,
I wake from my dream with my heart often weak.
My dreams are not sweet, my reality in denial,
in all your torment, still bring an immaculate smile.

I loved you.
Even if you never felt the same.

I'm fighting with my soul
when it calls out your name.

"Friends with Benefits doesn't include dental and health? Then NO."

"Silent Symphony"

A silent symphony has taken over my being.

My voice is silent, but my spirit is screaming.

You're here. My dream has arrived yet not come true.

You; with another while my heart is with you.

Beethoven and Mozart the only songs I can play.

For I must create my own words in order to silence my day.

My soul floating above my body and it will not rest,

As long as my heart is living outside of my chest.

I cannot describe my weakness though strength has no pride.

To tell you I love you again, I'd rather go hide.

Behind a smile, and a friendship that began as a romance,

A relationship unlabeled. A solo slow dance …

To an up-tempo beat,

My once steady swing dance met you and landed with two foreign feet.

I do not know this dance, but I will not claim defeat.

At mercy to be in your presence, my reflection in your eyes, and my name in your speak.

Beethoven and Mozart are the only songs I can stand,

As I sit in the rain dreaming of holding your hand.

Again.

Fear, anticipation, and memories of how we were,

I see you from a distance, and you show up with her.

My soul floating above my body and it will not rest

As long as my heart is living outside of my chest.

Heavenly experience without the stigmata,

Forever imprinted as my moonlit sonata.

"Lezbehonest"

I watch you from afar on many occasion.
Though you may not realize your words persuasion,
to my curiosity's invasion, because I think you're amazing.
I often find myself gazing, even if it is wrong,
I see lyrics in your eyes, and they write me a song;
that I sing, when I hear your voice in passing.
Wondering if I'm the only one whom envisions
the two of our bodies clasping...

Gasping...for air, because I don't think we will pace,
ourselves with the chemistry, the fire, the flare...
But it's fair, that I be honest, whether anyone else approves,
I'm in awe with each curve of femininity as I watch you move.

For when you move, your body has a rhythm that only you can create,
Each meticulous shape, paralleling my awe with a need for heartbreak....
Because I don't think you'll take, this invitation, of femininity combined,
as you speak with your heart and I see through your mind.
As my heart beats and I feel the pulse through my being,
as you come into view, with your vibe, before I am seeing.
I watch you from afar on many occasion.
Though you may not realize your words persuasion,
to my curiosity's invasion, because I think you're amazing.

While I recite I am intently gazing,
admitting...
I see lyrics in your eyes, this song to you I compose,
Lezbehonest for a moment as I indecently propose...

"I'm not saying I'm Banksy. I'm just saying no one has ever seen me and Banksy in the same room together..."

"Damn"

I laid in her spot for a few days without knowing...
It was her dick that I was in the passenger seat blowing.

He had me open like a stargazer lily that finally had bloomed.
I gave him my purity.... without caution.. I gave in too soon.

Because I felt a connection I had never before.
He kissed me with passion and made me want more...

With an ear and a mouth that made sense to my own.
His spirit, his voice, his essence left my mind blown.

I learned a valuable lesson ... and to him I see what I am.
I'm a mistress... Involuntarily... My heart is now damned.

Damn.

"Chivalry isn't dead. It's just locked in the closet with a ball gag and handcuffs; while being serenaded by a man wearing Rambo attire as he repetitiously sings his rendition of 'In the Air Tonight'..."

"Verse 6"

Absent of magic, I; no magician. I have no tricks.
My word. My love; all I have Is this.
Be my Matthew Chapter 19 Verse 6.

Sincere without intention; my free will has been possessed.
I see you with my spirit
as it peeks from underneath my flesh.

Unaware I was; for I sought nothing,
when you came into my view;
Discernment spoke and made sure I was awake when I found you...

Where I stand, looking you in the eyes and holding your hand on a faithful path.
Just yesterday I told God a combination of your essence did not exist.
I didn't hear him when he laughed.

You are the 'Prototype" beyond 3000, past, present, all other men.
Be my Lover. Be my Brother. Be my Adam. Be my Friend.

Absent of magic. No magician. No flash. No insincere tricks.
Full of love. Unconditionally.
Willing to grant your *every* wish;

Matthew Chapter 19, Verse 6.

"If I told you"

If only this were another life, and perhaps of other kin.
If I asked you to kiss me, would you do it again?

If I were the keys, and you the Piano Grand,
Would you allow me to hold your song to my hand?

Would you stand or invite me to sit in your lap,
Would you hear the ovation inside me, even if I froze to clap?

Would you allow your voice to echo inside of my skin?
If I asked for an encore, would you please me again?
Perhaps as a friend, a lover in hiding,
Pretending not to see you as my lip bleeds from biting.
If I told you I longed to run my fingers through your hair,
That I was not selfish, that YOU I would share.

Would you hold it against me and my recent liberation,
If I told you your eyes inspired masturbation.
The way you move moves through me, though you're not within reach.
Embarrassed, aroused as you are reading my speech.
Guilt stricken by my sudden inappropriate craving,
Feeling possessed by sound as my spirit is aching.

To have YOU, just once, your heartbeat upon my breasts,
To hear your voice as your teeth gently graze my chest.
If only this were another life, and perhaps of other kin,
Ashamed for in my mind I may have committed a sin.

Wanting to dance on top as your fingers ice skate upon the ivories,
Hoping my eyes don't give away my forbidden secret fantasy.
If I were the keys, and you the Piano Grand,
Would you allow me to hold your song to my hand?

Would you stand or invite me to sit in your lap,
Would you hear the ovation inside me, even if I froze to clap?
Anything I would give, to simply hold your hand,
If I were the keys, you'd be the piano grand.
Play me...

"Cruise"

Reminiscent; of a moment only you can enable me to relive.
Encrypted; yet unlocked the 'Davinci Code' in my heart so that I would let you live.
And you do... As if it was restructured with new cells to be powered by you.

A new shape, a new hue, your presence alone has me moved.
Outside and beside of myself; my smiling reflection confused.
Because we're afraid of being misused, you're un-accused.
My heart beats your rhythm; my soul sings your blues.

There's no other YOUS, nothing even close,
You've been in my life for mere months but I FEEL you the most.
Questioning destiny's possibilities as I raise to a toast,
A new me has emerged; should I hold back or am I supposed—-
To. Love. You.

A chemistry I'm sure I won't find anywhere else,
When you're inside of me; I'm inside of myself.
You're the fire to my fire, the water to my well,
I'm standing on two feet while flying, yet I know that I fell.

This is just a promise to love you with only this moment's expectation.
A love letter in song; with no return address,
Just a "For Your Information".
My heart beats your rhythm; my soul sings your blues,
You're the smoke to my blunt; and I just want to 'Cruise'...

"If I had a tail, it would wiggle when you came into view.

#RejectedGreetingCards "

"Synchronicity"

Synchronicity defined: "the experience of two or more events that are apparently casually unrelated occurring together in a meaningful manner."

Absence of a physical presence that may not exist,
Absence of the possibility that my forehead you might kiss.

With thy lips, that spoke words to me that you never knew.
Before you I was aware of the birds but unaware that they flew.

Presence of your soul when I know you're nowhere near.
Presence of your eyes in those of strangers, except the one in the mirror.

I hear her, her eyes reflect a loss of what almost was…
Her delusional memory, the prelude to a dream- the prologue to us.

Since meeting you my heart developed a new rhythm,
A synchronicity that I cannot find, 7,000 miles away I've lost my mind.

In a city I have never been but am willing to search until I find you again,
Forcing distractions, sitting still when like a pinwheel I spin.

It's raining in my heart even if you left your umbrella,
The thunder in my soul shakes the walls of my cerebellum.

Convincing myself of insanity for being sure that you're the one,
Lies told to ourselves tend to be those that are fun.

Searching for your eyes in the eyes of strangers, except the one in the mirror,
She came when you appeared, I disappeared, I fear her.

Absence of a presence that created a life within.
Absence of my love. Absence of a friend.

A synchronicity I cannot find, miles away in a city I've never been.
Living for the moments, the dreams, and to see you again.

Presence of your soul when I know you're nowhere near.
Presence of your eyes in those of strangers, except the one in the mirror.

"Stockholm Syndrome"

Forgive me if he turns out to be Satan.

He can have my soul if he asked.

Resistance I reckon; a thing of my past.

Submissive; I have mastered well and become,

Obsessed with his happiness and making him cum.

Fiery passion is obsessed with me.

I; controlled by force that I cannot see.

Forgive me if he turns out to be Satan.

Unspoken I promised that I would die waiting.

On him, and the return of the butterflies capable of flying through fire,

Carrying a passion I never want fulfilled, I crave to desire.

Him;

and his return, the tease of his selfish kiss.

Sometimes unsure if he even exists.

Or does he live in my imagination,

A psychotic source of demented brain elation.

A willing hostage I have become,

Obsessed with his happiness and making him cum,

to me.

Pretending not to care, yet pining with ache for his embrace,

His cinnamon scent, his angelic face.

I'm not sure if I chose, nor do I remember being taken captive,

Unless an arrow with poison plagued my heart with his acid.

In the instant, he walked into my view,

My blood went warm and my vision was hued.

Perhaps I am sickened, by chance willingly bitten,

Under a holistic spell, virginally smitten.

No weapon in sight, whether secret or blatant,

Forgive me if he turns out to be Satan.

"BASS"

It was a pleasant surprise when I looked in his eyes; unplanned and unexpected,

As if during his stare and clasp of the strings; we made love; ears unprotected.

Bass; the rhythm you feel deep in your core, falling in sync with your heart and altering its beat,

With my ears I saw him, with my eyes I decided to speak.

Me lost in the crowd yet seeing only **TWO** instruments on stage;

The one in his grasp and the one I'm sure *slayed*...

During persuasion by music, finesse, and effortless skill,

I found my motives being shifted without my free will.

As if during his stare and clasp of his strings;

The phallic symbol foreshadowed my moans and my screams.

I long for the beat; my sustenance and my addiction,

The **BASS** wanted to move me so I give it **permission**.

"Falling in love with the wrong person is like eating hot pizza. The roof of your mouth may be missing now, but it was delicious & fun."

"HAD"

When what you have becomes what you had.
When my smiles become the reason your ass is sad.

When you told me I wasn't enough, and I gave you my all.
When you saw me flying, you told me you'd rather me fall.
When I changed my life to mold your desire,
you brought a match and set mine to fire.
When you were a star to me before your narcissi fame.
When I became blind yet I saw that you'd changed.

When the groupies came, ...when the spotlight was on.
I tried to stand beside you, but pushed behind you, till gone.

When my tears spoke what my mouth could not.
When my heart broke, I rather it be shot.

When your number one fan becomes the last on your list.
I was the first one in line, for your ass to be kissed.
I wanted you minus the clothes, the flash, and bull shit.
Minus the cars, the wheels and the tricks...
tricks, and stunts, road trips and full blunts.
I was a freak for you, but you'd rather those sluts.
When I was myself, and you were an imposter.
You were my only, and I was lost on your roster.

When I lay down at night, and I see your face;
My dream is a nightmare, no saving grace.
For you had a taste, of what love really was,
but you wanted emptiness, you didn't want love.
When you lie, you're a con, and the whole world believes.
When the truth comes to light, it will be you that's deceived.
I'm moving on, don't call me. Your voice makes me mad.
When what you have becomes what you had...
When you're no longer able to perform the stunts and the tricks.
When no longer is anyone swinging from your dick.
When you become you, minus the flash and bull shit...
When no one is in line for your ass to be kissedwhen you wake up and
you remember how you treated me and that makes you sad...

When what you have is NOTHING like what you once HAD...

"I don't mind being vulnerable and therefore shamelessly honest. It's being passive and biting my tongue for too long that I regret."

"Infinite Lust"

You've got me on a plateau that I've never thought I could reach.

You're adding to my lyrics yet stuttering my speech.

I want to allow you to teach, me, the art of seduction.

I'm at witness to your protection but I crave an abduction,

An orgasmic eruption, as you walk into view,

I want to fuck, taste, tease every brown inch of sweet you...

Willing to be used for your pleasure at depths you've never peaked,

Craving every erotic fantasy, every arousal, every leak.

Talk dirty to me, let me be-your porn star, your every wish

Like you were a wet dream, I cream with each kiss.....

Take advantage of my virgined moment of infinite lust.

The descriptive memory of you sends my loins thru a rush.

My mind and body in a blush, I feen for your touch,

Curious how one had made the sober into a lush?

You're the Heroin, the Cocaine of the dicks that I've fucked,

I'm addicted to your body, my hormones have ran muck.

I want to fuck, taste and tease every sweet inch of you.

An orgasmic eruption, as you walk into view.

A lust like no other, I'm at your dispose.

My mind had no choice, my body has chose.

"MoNSTeR"

Dear Young Woman, Beautiful in and out;
Forgot what TRUE LOVE was all about...
He hurt you, thru his screams, and sometimes he'd shout.
He'd slam the doors, with accusations all about.
Starting arguments with you just so he could cheat.
While you waited at home, with no food to eat.
Within just a few months, your face now looks old,
though tears have dried, your heart growing cold.

Dear Young Woman, Please don't weep.
I pray that tonight you will get some sleep.
I hope tonight he doesn't come,
and threaten you with one in the chamber from his gun.
Though you have tried many times to leave,
you're losing hope and no longer believe.
Though you didn't do the harm, you go t the black eyes
Though you told the truth, you were served a dish of lies.
Now looking in the mirror at someone you don't recognize,
because he tore you down mentally, and constantly criticized.

Dear Young Woman, He's gone out of your life;
but you miss this monster, whom in your heart, left a knife.
Please my sweet, as I pray for your heart,
Keep it guarded so you don't fall apart.
Don't envy the next woman you see him entertain,
He wouldn't do you right, so you'll be another's gain.

Dear Young Woman, Beautiful, smart and full of love,
Hold your head high, and you'll get all you dream of.
He hurt you thru his screams, and sometimes he'd shout
Love does not hurt or break you. Let that Monster OUT.

"Do it. Get carried away. Just not by security."

"Unicorn"

His name is "Temptation"; he wants me as his mistress.
He wants my scent to follow him & his boxers painted by my lipstick.

Temptation stands before me, and his red apple looks delicious.
He's become my Genie, and for me he's promised infinite wishes.
If only for my kisses and secret rendezvous of passion;
pretending untempted yet delight shivers imagining us thrashing.
Temptation; wrapped in a shiny package and topped with a bow,
I longed for your presence and now up you show.

Her name is "Beware"; for her eyes reveal she knows his plan,
She shakes my hand and knew before I did that I would crave her man.

Beware watches us with precise scorns in her deep brown eyes,
she pictures Temptation's head between hers and then quenched thirst between MY thighs.
Beware imagines her and I sharing identical moments with Temptation,
She imagines if I were to fulfill him would he leave their situation?
Leaving her at home in solo masturbation?

PERHAPS.
Images of us naked together flash through the mind of Temptation,
Beware is aware, sees the same image, now also curious for a relation….ship…with me …

For I am the Unicorn, Temptation wasn't sure existed.
I'm in his memory as he foreshadows and psychically reminisces.
My name is "Forbidden"; for I am the fruit which stiffens his tree.
I beckon him by simply existing, TEMPTATION longs for me….
Forbidden and unaware he had room to feed an imagination,
as I now LUST for him too and EVERY "SIN-SATION".

She wants to play with my apples, and also wants me as her mistress,
He wants my secret rendezvous and boxers painted with my lipstick.
Being the other woman, to a woman and a man.
Infinitely playing with "Danger" in the palm of three hands.
Beware of Temptation and the Unicorn that's Forbidden,
Fantasies become Nightmares when Agendas are Hidden.

"Dear You"

Dear You,

I cannot pretend you don't exist now that I know that you do,

The moment you spoke, I lost myself in your YOU...

I cannot show you what you aren't ready to see,

Cannot make you stop loving her, and start loving me.

I cannot make this make sense to you, or even myself,

But I realized something the moment you left—

You were a stranger that my heart knew so well,

You're no magician, yet I'm under your spell.

Willing to be everything that you need,

If you take off your blinds and decide to SEE me.

I see you. I see you in perfection flawed in direction.

I see you with my soul, I feel your reflection.

Awed at my capacity and intensity to feel,

Questioning my mind for what my heart knows is real.

If a friend I must be, then that role I will take,

For your absence would cause my heart to break.

As I listen to your heart break, I hear the echo of my own,

For I am now lost, because now mine you own.

My heart merged to yours when you held me so tight,

Afraid, Nervous, and Ashamed to tell you last night.

The moment you spoke, I lost myself in your YOU...

I cannot pretend you don't exist now that I know that you do,

If I must be a fool, allow this fool to be true,

I can, do, and will be in love with you.

 Seems with love I'm always playing tag,

I placed my heart in your carry -on bag.

A friend.

"Between Blinks"

Caught in the moments;
where we briefly lock eyes.
Captive by thought-
hiding my "idea" between my thighs.
Blood Rushing away
from my roaring heartbeat.
I'm afraid of our silence
Because within its empty sound,
I hear the rest of me speak.
Nervous, I become,
wondering if you hear me.
Aware my subconscious will dominate my actions
if I let you come near me.
I need you to fear me,
and stay out of arms reach.
I'd rather be submissively strong,
than incredibly weak.

Watching your lips and your eyes,
and hoping you aren't reading my body language;
as I struggle to be stoic
and fail to conceal my body's anguish.
Timid I seem,
dismissing respectful eye contact;
as I daydream BETWEEN BLINKS
of you on your back.
Just days ago, I knew how to act,
Intrigued now to touch you,
IMAGINE THAT.
Imagine if I had said "yes"
to my inhibitions.

I'd be free from writing
living instead of just wishing.
Instead of throbbing,
we could be sweating,
But this is complicated….
so I can't be letting…. You…
Catch me in the moments
where we briefly lock eyes.
Nor let you capture the idea
I've hid between my thighs.
Still afraid of our silence
because within it I hear our bodies speak.
I'm becoming submissive,
finding strength in my weak… Moment.
Nervous, and prepared
Just in case you by chance hear me,
Allowing my subconscious to dominate my actions
if I let you COME NEAR ME.

"There's a silent joy in knowing that your X still masturbates to your pictures, lubed with his tears."

"A.K.A. Richard"

Something is missing, ever since I made you leave,
I contemplate the season I made you the air that I breathe.
I reminisce of love and see how it was,
I'm aware of the miracle and the damage it does.
I see a smile that you flooded with a fury of tears,
I can feel that moment that took away all our years.

Something is missing, ever since I last kissed your face.
I contemplate your presence alone, making my heart race.
I reminisce of love; the deepest ever fathomed,
I'm aware of your spell and in awe with your tandem.
I see a girl; naive with a heart that is full,
whom she freed upon a boy whom was full of BULL-

SHIT, was what you fed me when I was hungry for sincerity,
an agape attachment immaculate detached by your ignorant severity.
Something is missing,
ever since you were last inside me,
I was so OUTSIDE OF MYSELF
that my own soul stood behind me.
I reminisce of love;
and the prison you left me in.
I would have gave you my life
You weren't even a good friend.

I see a smile, I lost,
when I let you shake my world,
I see Riedells, I see Rims,
I see a weak ass S-Curl.
I realize what I miss,
not you or your SHIT,
But I hate that you fit,
as I come to the conclusion….
I just miss your "DICK"….
"AKA Richard"

"Happily Apathetically Ever After"

Open your chest to kiss you on your heart.
Open your brain to place myself in your thought.
Open my hands to ensure you safe landing.
Open my arms to place you in, above, and under my standing.
Open my legs to give you the highest form of pleasure found on this planet.
Open my body to allow you to consume it, until we can no longer stand it.
Irony; when in the absence of reason can be a bitch,
With certainty aware I do not deserve this.

Open my hands to ensure you safe landing.
Open my arms to place you in, above, and under my standing.

Apathetically jaded, in the absence of reason.
Emotionally masturbated to keep from joy's grieving.
Leaving my heart in a place even I cannot find it,
Perhaps this time will keep Satan from attempting to blind it.
I was ready to love you even though I was afraid. I really wish you would have stayed.
You gave love and attention you paid. Forehead kisses and hugs gone away.
But hey, I didn't have you anyway. In the seventh hour I gave my love to you.
I allowed your wings to pierce through my skin and within my hole you flew.
I was a fool in the seventh hour as I let you place your body inside of mine.
☐
The numbing sensation over my whole body ensures this will be my last time.

Open my legs to give you the highest form of pleasure found on this planet,
Open my body to allow you to consume it, until we can no longer stand it.

Foolish I was as I envisioned you were the exception.
Now afraid of myself for I was the hand of my heart's deception.
I held the gate open, I let the thief in. I am capable of doing it again. Or am I?
Have I yet become jaded? Jaded enough that I can say that love is apathetically hated?

Do I want a callus where my heart used to be, or still crave love in some form molded for me?
My fear is that one day I will wake up and the once hidden scars will be surfaced for all to see.

Open your chest to kiss you on your heart,
Open your brain to place myself in your thought.

The love of family, friends, and strangers, chased now eludes me,
Even those of blood would rather confuse than consume me.

Apathetically jaded, because there's a hole in my chest cavity where wind now blows.

Opened metaphorically transformed, and now I am CLOSED.

"Moan"

Silence has a way of telling on your thoughts,

Even when you pray you won't get caught...

So I taught...my words to confuse my listener

I made an oath as a subliminal minister-

But I was caught off guard to his sublime nature,

I found paradise in his eyes and wanted to ride his elevator-

All the way to the bottom before we reached the top,

Confident dehydration would kill me for I'd ever say stop-

To him...

To him... the most beautiful man I've ever seen with all of my eyes,

The set that you see, and the set that I hide.

He walked away, and I never got the chance- to be with him alone...

But the moment I saw him, he made me whisper a "moan".

"Those whom speak negatively behind you, are already in the perfect position to kiss your ass."

"Broken Glass"

He said it was an emergency, so she let him break the glass,
She thought he was being a gentleman, since he at least asked.

Unlike the last who intentionally moved things too fast,
unhitched his pants and showed his whole ass.

Perpetuating prayer, wearing a cross, and praying in mass,
water isn't the only thing that mirage's favor; it's a love that will last.

He said he was different, he would be unlike all of the rest,
called her his Princess and claimed he'd love her best.
He sang her sweet melodies, sent roses, she witnessed him tell God that with her he was Blessed.
He wrote her love songs with his eyes when he sang into her breasts.
Pretending the whole time that he was sincere and there was no jest,
until the night I awaited him and his X called me and confessed.

She said it was an emergency, so I let her break the glass,
she said he was now HER gentleman,
said she was the reply to the questions he asked...
Unlike the last, who intentionally moved things too fast.
she said he unhitched her pants.

THEY broke a heart, and she gave him her ass.

"Intuition; please forgive my naïveté, for my heart often screams louder than your whispers."

"Omissions"

On a cloud I do not recognize,

A plateau I've never been,

A mountain I'm willing to climb,

A race I plan to win.

My imagination in a daze,

Of combining saint with sin,

 Knocking on yours

Hoping that you'll let me in.

But when?

Time is of the essence,

Yet I eagerly daydream,

About making my silence heard,

And making my insides scream.

Believe me if you must,

For my words have no omissions,

Until I can reach around your cloud,

While you dominate my submission.

I have no I.V.

As you're swimming through my veins,

You have no dungeon,

Yet I place myself into your chains.

Saying it sweetly, albeit discretely,

Every part of my being craves you completely. ...

To be within me,

places of my body, dimensions of my mind,

Use your body as a flashlight to tell me what you find...

As you open both my thighs

As your fire enters my eyes,

As we reach the highest plateau

On this cloud I do not recognize...

"Tantric"

Enamored with his torment, I pine for his presence,
I, find myself, mentally lusting, for his existence...
I yearn for him, and he compels me...
Caution to the wind, craving him to unveil me.
I'm ardently tempted, and don't mind the sweet sin.
Captivated, in every capacity, hoping desire won't end.
Nothing last eternal, especially lust for a friend.
He's bewitched me -at his mercy for his zen...

His Zen, his energy, I must have....as I enjoy the chase.
I'm unconventional and for him I must wait.
My conscious mind, so eager, for anything he gives.
Addicted to his touch...and the part of me that lives...
that somehow he seems to find,
as he looks through my eyes to see to my mind.
With such simplicity, and genuine discipline...
I'm in awe, at mercy, and fiend for his ZEN.
Is he teasing me, or is this how he plays,
as I intricately walk through his mental maze.

He feeds every dimension of my complicated arousal that starts in my mind
for I am not easily wooed, Esoteric, yet free spirit-undefined.
I'm aware and awakened at the heightened of my knowing,
intrigued by this soul, whom without touch, sends my mind blowing.
I'm glowing, with a blush, that sears through my bronze skin...
His torment, his pleasure, as I cave for his Zen.

"I've a new crush; The Pumpkin Spice Latte. How do I know it's serious? I swallowed."

"The End"

I can't make you take me places, or introduce me to your family.
I can't tell you that you are supposed to do these things gladly.
I cannot make you feel guilty, or give you "those eyes"...
I can't make you understand, the disappointment you gave with your lies.
I cannot make you show up; when you say that you'll come.
I can't get back those years, when we should have had fun.
I can't tell you we have so many things in common, and so much to share.
I cannot get mad at you anymore, though you treat me unfair.
I won't wait anymore, I will move on after this.
I won't tell you about all that you will miss.
I won't cry, I won't need to reflect after I write,
I waited for you to show up, for the last night.
I wanted to know you, you'll never know what you had.
And I'll never know, what it means to have a real DAD.

"I was playing his album while ignoring his text messages. I like his music but he's an asshole."

"That Day"

Open your heart she said unto me,
Give him your love and Get what you need.
Then in return he will provide,
A love within and on the outside.
Be honest; Give him your all,
Be subservient and wait for his call.
Then in return you will be his queen,
Be comforting whenever he's mean.
Tell him your secrets and all your desire;
Give him your heart and light to his fire.
Then in return you will receive,
A love no other will ever believe.
Don't ask questions, she continued to say,
"Be a good woman, don't stand in the way.
Then in return he'll be honest and true,
He'll feel the freedom and he will love you."
I opened my heart because she said,
I went home one day, she lay in my bed.
Then in return, he kissed her breasts,
My heart shattered inside my chest.
I gave him my love as he made love to her,
As I cried, my eyes were a blur.
Then in return they never saw me stand.
I stood and watched my friend with my man.
I was honest and gave him my all.
I came straight home when he didn't call.
Then in return, he didn't answer the phone.
I was his comfort. I thought he was alone.
I never asked questions, as I watched them dance bare.
I was a good woman to just stand and stare.
Then in return, I remembered her say,
  "be the love of his life, don't stand in the way."

I was in her way of fucking my man.
I grasped HARD, to the vase in my hand.
Then in return, I let them be free.
They had no comment when they finally saw me.
I gave to them, the vase that I held.
My heart broke and my soul yelled.
Then in return I clenched my vase,
and smacked the bitch across her face.
I opened my heart as I watched her bleed.
I was quiet; my man thought he could flee.
Then in return I threw him cut glass,
As I sliced his naked black ass.
I was subservient; and didn't stand in the way.

I had a vase because, he sent roses that day.

"You've been in Las Vegas too long when you're in the Buffet Line and looking for a VIP Host to bring you to the front."

"Fear and Awe. My favorite experiences seem to have these in common. Equally feeding off one another to prove the other right."

"Live Forever"

I'm going to live forever;
for this I have no choice.
Many won't be able to see me
until they hear my voice.

For some my voice is a whisper
While others hear my words as loud,
Yet being surrounded by many
doesn't mean you are ONE with that crowd.

I'm going to live forever,
You don't have to agree with my fate,
I've been here this whole time,
for those that think I'm late.

Enigmatic anomaly refusing the drugs THEY prescribe to me...
resisting the common thought processes that result in a prison purgatory,
so that we can live forever as extraordinary.

Cocky, never. My heart is heavy,
But I've learned to be strong so that I can carry,
this dream, this life, the vision that was put inside of me,
Until you feel my beat, you may not even see me.

I'm going to live forever,
in a place that has no rules,
No judges, no condemnation,
No opinions gave by fools.

There's a faucet of abundance that you can tap into if you choose,
Infinite possibilities ....

cause I. Refuse. To. Lose.

"Puente Hills"

They were louder than I was; the voices in your head,
they told you I didn't love you and blocked out things I said.
Instead I let my actions speak louder than my word,
but no matter what I did, that's not what you heard.

Over a cliff somewhere called the "Gateway" suspended in the air,
I picture green pastures full of angels and I see US there.
Cause that's where I visit you each time I close my eyes,
and the moment before I wake up, it never gets easier saying
"Goodbye".

Looking into your eyes, I saw there was trouble,
You told me you loved me and then pushed me out of your bubble.
I can still feel your heartbeat where you beckoned I lay,
You brought me close as you possibly could and then shoved me away.

How long did you drive, how long did you know?
Did you think about calling me or did you just go?

If I brought you the joy you claimed I brought to your world,
Then Cowboy why did you leave me, a cowboy-less cowgirl.

Your smile full of valleys that I traced with my fingertips,
from the mountains, to the ocean, to the Disneyland trip.

Scared. Cause I never felt safer in another human's air,
But now I'm unsafe and exposed cause you are not there.

Place your cowboy hat back upon my head,
The way that you did, when you said…
that they were louder than I was… the voices in your head.

GRATEFUL

About the Author

Khalilah Yasmin is an author and poet. She has her Bachelor of Science in Psychology. With a keen interest in human behavior, she enjoys the dichotomy between art and psychology as a medium to alter perceptions. Yasmin currently resides in Las Vegas, Nevada.

Twitter: @KhalilahYasmin
KhalilahYasmin.com

www.ingramcontent.com/pod-product-compliance
Lightning Source LLC
Chambersburg PA
CBHW070325100426
42743CB00011B/2568